LIFE
in the
PAST LANE

LIFE
in the
PAST LANE

POEMS

PETER CARLAFTES

THREE ROOMS PRESS

NEW YORK CITY

Life in the Past Lane
Poems by Peter Carlaftes

© Copyright 2023 by Peter Carlaftes

ISBN 978-1-953103-40-6 (trade paper original)
Library of Congress Control Number: 2023935237

TRP-107

Publication Date: September 26, 2023
First edition

BISAC Coding:
POE005010 POETRY / American / General
POE023010 POETRY / Subjects & Themes / Death, Grief, Loss
POE023000 POETRY / Subjects & Themes / General
POE023060 POETRY / Subjects & Themes / Political & Protest

COVER AND BOOK DESIGN:

KG Design International: www.katgeorges.com

DISTRIBUTED IN THE U.S. AND INTERNATIONALLY BY:
Publishers Group West: www.pgw.com

Three Rooms Press | New York, NY
www.threeroomspress.com | info@threeroomspress.com

To Max and Dylan

The poem, the song, the picture, is only water
drawn from the well of the people,
and it should be given back to them in a cup
of beauty so that they may drink
—and in drinking understand themselves.
FEDERICO GARCIA LORCA

CONTENTS

LIFE
in the
PAST LANE

YEAR OF THE EARTH PIG

twelve minutes into life–
my mom's aunt ran off
to fetch my dad
as I began there
in the Bronx

my dad was a bookie
yet he was working at
the Post Office then
to show a semblance
of legitimacy

twelve weeks into life–
cops broke down the door
to rip out the phone
from our apartment
on Valentine Avenue
which sowed mom's doubts
she'd learn to love him

pop moved us down the block
to a better place
with a different name on the lease
where he promised to give mom
all the things she quickly learned
she didn't want

twelve months into life–
my parents were divorced
though mom didn't have a clue
what it was she really wanted
outside of knowing
she didn't want pop

ME-TERNAL

my mother was born
to a marriage annulled
as her mother
discovered –that
her husband did time
for robbing a bank

their license was negated
by an edict from the church
although he did drag
my mom's Aunt Speranza
away from the asylum
where they were zapping her
with shock treatments
for being a wee bit off

not enough
for reinstatement
though
and
unluckily for mom
her mother's next
was not the same
once back from WWII

whereby my mom made
some poor choices too
along with my pop
whose poorest choice
unhappily
was her

MOMMY! MOMMY!

Mommy! Mommy!
I Want a Musket!

(Silence)

Repeat Demand

(Silence)

It's my constitutional right!
When do I get a musket?

(Silence)

Mommy! Mommy!
Why aren't you telling me
when I'll get my musket?

Because I've been dead
over 200 years–
As is your way of thinking

But Mommy
didn't the forefathers decree
that arming all men
would protect our way of life?

Mommy tries her best–
Why is it so damned hard
for you to understand
that finding the path toward peace
cannot be reached at the point of a gun

But what about foreign and domestic enemies?
What about another 9/11?
Or Weapons of Mass Destruction?

Get a grip!
You're almost Two Hundred and Fifty Years Old
for Christ's Sake –GROW UP!

Mommy! Mommy!
I Want A Musket!

(Silence)

The Supreme Court ruled that
the Second Amendment guarantees
an individual's right to own a gun

(Silence)

Mommy! Mommy!
I want a Musket!

Alright
Mommy Relents
Enough you whiny brat
Here–

No, Mommy
Not This Musket!
I Want One With a Bigger Magazine

NO DOT, NO COM

My grandpa told his kids
just how much
he hated Turks
after fighting in
the First Balkan War, then
after sailing to America
assimilating
life anew
he soon returned
to Europe
and fought in WWI
where the Germans
shelled him
with enough
mustard gas to
damage his lungs
and eventually
kill him
though
in between
he made ends
meet
for his family
as a florist

my Aunt said
in the mid 1930s
she'd climb up
to Tar Beach
and play a game
with her best friend
called
Kill The Turks

I don't recall
my pop
ever
calling out
the Turks, yet
he must've had
some hate
handed down

his best years
began
when he rejected
a prearranged
marriage, then
upon
learning the score
as a shill
out in Vegas
he bided time
driving mob guys
around
to different
poker games, until
he made his bones
as a bookie
in the 1950s
living large
while
taking bets

I was too young
to remember
my grandpa's
death

my first memory
came age 3

staring east
out the window
in pajamas
with a fever
watching this man
paint
a two-family
house
perched atop
one
hanging
scaffold, that
suddenly dropped
a few feet
to the right
tripping
him back
off the side

He fell
straight down
through
a spiked
iron fence
and I cried
to my pop
That man's
dead

my pop looked out
the window
as the police
arrived
quickly
since
the 46th precinct
was right up
the block
then led me
over
to the couch
and turned
cartoons
on the TV

My pop
was wearing
pajamas too

just lazing
around
taking
bets on
the phone

he never
got dressed
before noon

I thought about
that poor man
who died from
doing his job
and

now
I think about
my pop, who
later told me
how
when I was born
he had to work
at the Post Office
and even though
he paid off
the timekeepers
and most of
the others there
were feeding
him bets
supervisors
came around
every so often
and
he'd have to
show up
to work for
two weeks

later on
he'd always say
those two weeks
almost killed him
and
also thinking now
they eventually
did

FEEL FOR THE STREET

you'd run into certain guys
in different parts of town

maybe Mikey in the park
then Reggie on Lex
later Tony near the Village
and inconceivably
there were (somehow)
TWO Arties with a gimp
one Eastside, one West

Artie East had red hair
and a knife hid in his cane
you could always spot him
bobbing through the crowd

and if anybody needed
a deuce or a fin
one of us
would always
stake the other

though
once in a while
you'd spot a guy
who owed you
cross the street

and of course there were some
you would never see again
but as a rule
we never welched
and if we

didn't have
the cash
we had a story

one night
starving
I met a kid
Curtis
who said
Follow me

we didn't have
a dollar
between us

after dodging
around through
the bustling
crowd
we strolled
into Tad's
on Times Square
which made
very little sense
since
you had to pay
first
before eating

well
my new found friend
grabbed a tray
and told the cook
medium rare
so I did the same

signing Two
all the while
eyeing Curtis
who wasted no time
once the cook
set our steaks
on two plates

he snatched them up
with his hands
and galloped
straight out
the front door
leaving me
to match the pace
right behind him

we dashed
along 7th
turning left
on 45th
where we
stood between
parked cars
gnawing down
our stolen meat

parting ways
soon after that
with a smile

I jumped a turnstile
to the Bronx
where my
furnished room
awaited

at the mercy of
each element
so few of which
were kind

MY SOUL TO KEEP

I snuck down the stairs
in the quiet of night
with a torn, stained pillowcase
stuffed with torn, stained clothes
cause I didn't have the rent
for the week gone by

then I sat on a bench
with my torn, stained lot
and could think of
no better place to be

until I found a car
on Fordham Road
that seemed more
abandoned than me

its windows
were shattered
the back seat
inviting

I put my head down
on that
pillow of clothes
which I left in the car
the next day –once awoke
while i went off
to hustle some food

this was four days of life
till a friend dropped by
and gave the word
that Richie moved out
from Duke's up the block
so the couch was mine
for fifty a month

so –enterprising
young man that I was
bummed a buck
to buy a subway token
and took the train
down to Times Square
where I worked the door
of some massage parlor
handing out flyers
for four bucks an hour
paid cash
at the end
of the night

twelve hours later
I climbed five flights
to pay Duke the fifty
and had a place for a month

then the very next day
walking down to the park
I saw that damned car
had its street side smashed in
by some hit'n run drunk
in the middle of the night

where I once was –wow
would've been me

guys were laughing
should've been
ha ha ha
though it wasn't

there was luck
yet no why

the next week
I watched
as they towed off
that car
then turned
up my street
sighing
here comes
that five flights
of stairs

UNEASY GO

Kung Fu Willie gave me
a handful of pills

I asked him about the yellow ones
he told me they were neutralizers
adding
the speckled were light ups

I swallowed them down
with a warm 7up

Crazy Dennis
followed suit

Willie chuckled
cause he knew
and we didn't

Kung Fu Willie
back two years
from Vietnam
got his name
because he held
some degree
of black belt
and once sparred
with Bruce Lee

me and Dennis
left Willie's
for the Patio
on Webb
joining
some pals
who were
smoking
a joint

Buddy
gave the joint
to Jemise
who took a hit
then passed it
to Angel
who tried
to walk off
but Phil
got it back
had a toke
then handed it
to Black Carl

I sat next to
Black Carl
who
held out
the joint
then
everything
around me
went dark

The next thing
I knew –smoke
cleared
all around
where
a black hand
still held out
a joint

I was taking
a hit, when
some cartoon cop
pointed
absurdly shrieking
They're smoking
marijuana
right here

when I realized
that we were in
the 46th precinct
I quickly
ate the joint
and blew
another fuse

I heard
What's your name
as the smoke
cleared again
but not knowing, I
didn't answer

having lost my
shoes, socks, belt
shirt, wallet, keys
all I had left on
were my jeans

no money, ID

the next time
they called me
Pete
Is that your name
Pete

I nodded
Yes

the cops said
they found me
inside a hospital
up on a desk
trying to rip a clock
from the wall

I had a cigaret
but when I went
to take a drag
it wasn't there

I looked around

a doorknob
followed
my gaze
up the wall
where
a gargoyle
with fangs
was fluttering
its wings
by the
fluorescent
fixture

my head
took its time
but I
finally
came down
in the Summer
of '75

and now
after years
of my tussle
with why
that clock
on the wall
still remains
out of reach

POEM AWAY FROM HOME

Beatnik O found me sitting in the park
and bid I'll write you a poem for a buck

But, I pushed back
You wrote me one last week
for only fifty cents

he said Sold
and began his creation
there in Central Park
on a summer afternoon

didn't have the heart
to tell him I was broke

he calmly looked me in the eye
while handing me his piece
easing Don't worry, Kid
You can owe me

SOLID AS A ROCK

the Earth froze
in an instant
circa 1977
mid-dance
Disco Inferno

discovered years later
by a distant breed
who studied the cut
of the bell bottom cloth
and the weight of
the platform shoe
and quickly came
to the conclusion
that this bunch
was headed for
extinction regardless
so the mishap of freezing
right there in mid-step
was a much kinder fate
than they deserved

BACK RENT BOOGALOO

just the day before
I had toiled 10 hours
with a hangover so nasty
it could've cut through steel

climbing warily up and down
a daunting thirty-foot ladder
hacking dead fronds
from myriad palm trees
on different properties
for the landlord
who stood there watching
but at least I made up
the back rent I had incurred
when my roommate Jack
got stuck out of town
with his half of the dough

so when I got home
I called Steve in construction
and asked if he had any work
to which, unfortunately
Steve answered Yes
they were starting a new job
tomorrow at 5am

this was Tucson, Arizona
where I moved to on a whim
because I had family there
and you started work early
outdoors

then just when I hung up
after telling Steve I'd show
Jack came home looking
like a beast from the wilds
and even though I was flush
cause he paid off his rent
I had given my word
and was stuck −so
there I stood
the very next morning
at 5am
staring at a backhoe
that would soon
turn hard ground
into the makings of
a medical plaza
quickly deciding
regardless of rent
or a 30-foot palm
I just couldn't do this
again

I went home
and dragged Jack
out of bed and
drove him back
to the site
said my goodbyes
and for reasons unknown
took the next right
instead of going straight
where a car pulled out
from a bank parking lot

smack into me –crunch
went the front right fender
of my yellow Karman Ghia
and bang went my head off
its newly cracked windshield

the woman who hit me
was full of regret, and
suddenly
cops were everywhere

minutes later
Steve drove by
pulling over when
he recognized my car
and I danced around
joyously
She's Gonna Pay
and a few days later
her insurance did
and I didn't work a job
for the rest of that year

one crazy moment
I had to say no
then the Gods answered me
You have made the right choice

those were glorious days
sleeping in after that
hearing birds sing
such beautiful songs

RIGHT BY A FRIEND

Me, Tim, and Jack
were down in Nogales
swilling tequila
for most of the day

we each brought
a bottle back
of cheap Cuervo Gold
but sadly Tim slipped
and his bottle shattered
which really rattled Tim
who was driving

some silly cop
nailed us
five miles north
clocking poor Tim
at a hundred

the cop told us Tim
was going to jail
–adding
One of you has to drive
and since Jack
had no license
the winner was me
and right there the cop
gave me Tim's keys

Where do we bail out our friend
I asked
while the cop
pushed Tim's head
through the door

Nogales jail
was his answer

As the sun went down
on the drive
back to Tucson
Jack and I moaned
about what shitty luck
also laughing, that
as drunk as I was
they gave me
the keys to Tim's car

We decided they had to
if they wanted the bail
and that was the game
for us to pay bail
which was exactly what
we were going to do
just as soon as we could
raise the dough, cause
Jack and I were broke
like Tim's bottle

back in Tucson
I called up Nogales
to learn that Tim's bail was
a hundred and ten bucks
so we started dialing
all of our friends
who were either tapped
or not home
and then, instinctively
I came up with Tracey
(my-sort-of-then-ex)
who'd recently mailed me
a Dear John letter
neatly written on
yellow legal notepad paper
that included the sentence
and I quote
You tell me you love me
but right now Pete
those words seem
very unreal . . .

yes –that Tracey!

we drove to her place
where I banged on the window

startled from sleep
she came to
and asked
Why are you here?
so I answered
Do you have any money?

Tracey did not, though
upon hearing the story
she astoundingly wrote me
a check that would bounce

me and Jack hit the road
straight back to Nogales
where the cop made clear
that they only took cash
son of a bitch
all to hell

I was seeing dinosaurs
on the highway back
and the sun was coming up
by the time we got home
–where I had an idea:

call my boss Dick
to see if he would
cash Tracey's check
that I wouldn't say
was bad
and when I called him at 9
Dick said Sure thing, Pete
Come meet me at the bank
and by 11:05
me and Jack were driving
back down to Nogales
with just enough gas
and the cash

arriving at the jail
I announced my intention
but the silly cop said
there wasn't any bail
so I warned him in advance
He'd better clear a path
cause I was crashing in
to break out my friend

another cop appeared
and quickly took the cash
then brought me around
to a dimly lit room
where I sat on a bench
while he filled out the forms

now about this time
another cop escorted in
some frightful-looking creep
in a blue jumpsuit
who sat next to me
and asked for a smoke

I held one out
then lit him up
and he sat there puffing
while peeking at me
from the corner of his eyes
that is until I'd had enough
so I asked the jailer
Who the fuck is this guy?

the cop's jaw dropped
That isn't Tim Fortman?

the creep would not have
said one word
then strolled out with me
had I let him

I growled
Throw this bum out
and bring me my friend

they brought out Tim
and cut us both loose

we drove back to Tucson
quite cheerful all the way
where we still had
those two bottles waiting
and Tim paid Tracey back
the cash to cover her check
and all was well
for a short spell of time . . .

though every so often
I wonder to myself
what happened to that guy
they brought out instead of Tim
but, mostly I think –What a time!

FIRST TIME FOR EVERYTHING

I drove straight
to Oregon
just to be
with her
and got a job
at the same
cannery
and
became
a sample
grader, but
they laid
most everyone
off due to
a poor pea
harvest year

then her bus
broke down
so we sold it
for scrap
and packed
our stuff
with two dogs
in my Toyota

we were young
and in love
without need
to know why

we
picked
maraschino cherries
one day
in the Dalles . . .

saw a friend
in Bend . . .

made a stop
at Crater Lake
then . . .

Jennifer, Shadow
Putt Putt, and I
were driving south
on Highway 1
approaching
Big Sur
with the sun
going down
so we pulled off
in a cove
where we
decided to
spend the night
when
this crazy biker
pulled up
revving his motor
like it was
a motorcross
competition

he soon sped off
and so we waited
to sprawl out
on the beach
until –Rev Rev
he returned

we split to Big Sur
where the fog
was so thick
I had to open the door
and look down
to see if we were on
the right side of the road
when –thump
there went
another raccoon

about five miles later
driving ten miles per
we were flooded by
a one-word flash
of neon –Vacancy

we settled in a room
with some sodas
and the dogs

left the fog
to our surroundings

sleeping soundly
through the night

OFF THE ROAD

driving back
to NYC
from Tucson
with Mark
whose ad
Heading east?
I answered
and another guy
paying
our gas fare
to Dallas

me –tooling along
in a Chevy Caprice
when I ran out of steam
about eight hours in
with the sunrise
ahead
west of Pecos

both of the guys
had been sleeping in front
so I woke up the stranger
next to me
and asked him
to finish
the drive
into Dallas

now this was
bare-ass Texas land
where the stranger
took the wheel
with nothing
in any direction

I fell asleep
within a minute
once the car
set in motion
but then
I felt a jolt

my eyes popped open
barreling through
an open field

i looked over at the driver
who was sleeping
at the wheel

I elbowed the guy
who came to
and hit the brakes
then sharply
told the stranger
Get in back

if not for that bump
we might've
gone on for miles
or else –until
maybe
hitting a steer

the stranger fell asleep
then I got us into Dallas
where the stranger
paid for gas
and we waved
happily goodbye
at which point
Mark took the wheel
driving north
to Texarkana

NOT ON MY WATCH

doubt very much
if I were lost
in some canyon
that a herd
of wild horses
would try to
approach me
and ingratiate
themselves

Here, Boy
they'd coax me
Let one of us
trot you over
to the nearest
fast food spot

no
they would each
hide in the hills
until I died
of starvation
never giving
even one inch
up of wild

mankind
is doomed
and rightfully so
as the landscape
prepares
for our fossils

STORM CENTRAL

one hot, sticky night
nineteen eighty-two
in the West U neighborhood
of Houston, fucking Texas
where Jennifer and I
had been married
Mayday past
we fell asleep
with both the windows
in our bedroom
wide open
to wake up
at some point
soaked to the skin
with a storm cloud
passing through

not overhead
mind you, but
right through the room

our pillows, sheets
mattress, and
rugs were drenched

the mattress took
six days to dry

and the dogs
my, our dogs
same look of
disbelief

I doubt if
they ever
forgave us

VODKA AND SNOW

Blizzard of '81
New York City

half-gallon
of Vodka

basement
on Charles Street

Mitch and I
dug in for
the night

the Vodka
didn't last

we hit the street
drunk and loose
looking for a cab
to take us
downtown

snow covered
damn near
everything

Mitch banged
through
the door of
the first bar
we passed

and began
yelling Mike
like a madman

Who was Mike

I rubbed
my coat sleeve
across
the plate glass
window
and saw Mitch
stagger up
to a table
and ask
this couple
if they knew
where Mike
was

the bartender
came around
and said
Mike's not here
pal, so
I quickly
stepped in
and led
Mitch out
the door

one if by cab
we made it
to Puffy's

well almost
to Puffy's

we got stuck
at a Snow drift
that me and Mitch
climbed while
in sight of
the bar

we sat down
on stools
and smiled
at Bandit
who wasted
no time
You are both
too far gone

on to Prescott's

a semi-truck
parked on
the alley
'hind Puffy's
looked
very appealing
all covered
with Snow

C'mon Mitch
I waved, then
we climbed
to the top

slurring some
old song
as we danced
arm in arm

this clown
across the alley
threw open
his window
yelling
Shut the fuck up

we pelted him
with Snowballs

he threatened to
call the cops

I screamed Call
the fucking cops
you prick
It'll take them
three hours
to get here

he slammed
the window
muttering
Go fuck
yourself

I motioned
to Mitch
Let's get him

we climbed
down
from
the truck
to break in
the building
and kill
that fuck
but the front door
was set with
two deadbolt locks
pretty formidable
security for
a couple of drunks

damn

I leaned
on the door

It swung open

we entered
the building
but couldn't
go up, so
the moment
led us down
to the
basement
instead
where
assorted tools
and studded
walls half

covered in
sheetrock
awaited

a frenzied
rampage
ensued

Mitch
punched his
fist through
a sheetrock
wall while
I grabbed
a sledge and
knocked out
studs

we tore
that basement
to pieces

though
needing a drink
in the very
worst way
we plowed up
the street
on to
Prescott's
who else
could've stood
but Manuel
at the stick

I said Vodka
and grapefruit
adding Two

Mitch downed
his drink
to run outside
and fill
his glass
with Snow

Vodka and Snow
he yelled
Two

everyone there
was completely
fed up
with the two of us
by closing time

the whole building
sighed when
we walked out
the door

standing
in two feet
of snow
between
Prescott's
and Puffy's
Mitch
figured out

he had
lost his keys

shit
I had
left mine
at home

so
staggering
back to
the bar
I fell flat
on my face
in the Snow
and somehow
stood up
with the keys
in my hand

dawn
was breaking

I held the keys
over my head
and squealed
Mitch
The Keys

we both just
fell backward
in a moment
forever

forever ended

we trudged
to the 1 train
where Snow
was even
falling
through
the air vents

Mitch
dangled
his legs off
the edge of
the platform

a group of kids
were talking tough
on the downtown
side

Mitch
screamed
out loud
You Punks
Ain't Shit
with a devilish
light in his eyes

the kids
were hooked

snowballs
whizzed by

miss
after miss

our
underground
carnival
where nothing
could touch
him . . .

throughout life
I always smile
when I think
about the keys

and the next day–

I'd rather not
think about

I'LL DRINK TO THAT

I got a job once bartending
in the Men's Card Room
at a Golf and Yacht club
where the members played gin
for five grand a hand
so I kept my eyes peeled
and poured their drinks strong
while waiting for the knock
of opportunities to come

this was Virginia Beach
1983

weekdays were best
with the bar to ourselves
but on weekends
the members
played golf with
their friends
and all of them
always ordered
lunch afterwards
so I had to barrel
fifty yards
across the club
for every tray
then back
to serve them food

most Saturdays
were exhausting
though there was one–

I was on
my fifteenth food run
focusing on
quitting time
being only
an hour away
when
the assistant manager
informed me that
I had to work a double

bartending
a private party
for none other than
Secretary of State
George Shultz
whom I had dubbed
The Beast of Bechtel

so I decided right then
to piss in his drink
no matter
how mindless
it seemed
and told as much
to my colleague
setting up the main bar
who must've
quickly
sold me out

because
the next time
I crossed
with a tray
full of food
the manager
superseded
his assistant
to let me know
I no longer
had to work
a double

and behind them
I could see
through the door
into their office
two guys in dark suits
looking through a file
from the cabinet
–probably mine
and more than likely
secret service

but I didn't get fired
at least not for that

they fired me
for nothing
a few months later
which really
ticked me off
to no end

I should've been fired
without question
for threatening to piss
in George Shultz's drink
so the next job
I applied for
that I knew
I wouldn't get —I
wrote on the application
after
Reason for leaving
last place of employment

Threatening to piss
in George Shultz's drink

and this always
still brings me
a laugh
to this day
but I wonder
how much
satisfaction
I would feel
if I had only kept
my mouth shut

IMPERMANENCE

every Sunday night
after working at the club
Dick and I would buy the racing form
then drop by the Queensborough Bar
to figure out Monday's triple in the 9th

Sunday was the only night
you could buy the form
a day in advance
so we thought we had an edge
though we lost every bet

earlier
we had decided
to skip this week
until, Dick
while staring out
at 1st Avenue
saw a guy drop
a ten dollar bill
and, of course
he ran out and
grabbed it

so we changed
our minds
and went
to the bar
this being
our lucky night
where we figured
the E-G-B triple

with a Bob Dunham
horse on top

I put Dick in a cab
and took another home
where I slept till noon

later, I went
to the OTB
and bet
the one dollar
triple box
E-G-B
and shuffled home
thinking
I was out twelve bucks

At 5:30 sharp
I dialed the OTB hotline
to hear the letters E-G-B

the triple paid
twelve hundred bucks

I hung up
and called Dick
his girlfriend sobbed
Y-Y-Y-es
I squealed
Put Dick on the phone
She cried out
Dick's Dead!

apparently
Dick rode that cab
to a card club
in the Bronx, then
when he got home
his heart went
just like that

I cashed my ticket
thinking
one day
we all lose

although –there
in the meantime
I hadn't lost
yet

BEYOND THE PALE

working at the club
on a long Friday night
during proms
usually meant
there'd be 600 plus
and on this one
we were
well onto plus
which meant kids
who had each paid
twenty-five bucks
for two watery drinks
and three feeble comics
but were loose in New York
at Dangerfield's Club
and we were stuck there
serving them

the Maître'd Bobby
who was built like a stretch
with a heart on its sleeve
had the last show seated
and the place was packed
including the boss

for whom
the definition
small-minded
was much too
generous–
unlike him

in fact
the story goes:

he started out
back in the '60s
playing bass
in night clubs
where he took home
rolls of toilet paper
ketchup bottles
and the like
hidden inside
his case
so after hitting the jackpot
once partnering with Rodney
he should've been one of the most
giving guys on the planet
instead of the tight wrench he was

case in point:

even though
the room was full
Bobby got busy
when he saw
the kid in the wheelchair
enter with a party of four

the boy had only
stubs for arms
and not much more
for legs

Bobby set him up
at the head of
table zero
right as the emcee
started the show
and I set him down
a blended fruit juice
that the girl to his right
helped him drink
with a straw

and right about then
the boss showed his face
which filled with suspicion
catching sight of that kid

he pulled Bobby aside
and demanded to know
How'd the kid pay
if he doesn't have arms

the look on Bobby's face
was one beyond disbelief

any decent owner
would've paid that party's tab
without giving it a thought
but ours was anything but

then later
long after
the boss had gone home
we sat around with drinks
while Willie the waiter
started telling a story
from the time he worked
The Living Room
which was usually
our cue to go home
but none of us on this night
could play out the bit
so we all heard Willie
recount how Tony Bennett
tipped him twenty whole dollars
again

LIFE IN THE PAST LANE

I locked up the bar on Lyon Street
and stared into the mist of a wannabe fog
thinking –Hey, it's really not so bad here
although it would take a lot more doing
to actually win me over–
moving from NYC to San Francisco
cities world's apart
and I was fighting the transition
when a portent appeared
first across Lyon Street
then from up the hill
unmistakably meant to help me
adjust to a new way of life

the scene began in a light mist
me walking to my car
a few parking spots
up the hill from the bar
when over the wall
of the Presidio
jumped two troubled bums
scaly beards and white skin

one saw me and snickered
sucking snidely in his breath
while the other bum there
screamed out Fuck you

so I popped my car's trunk
and yanked out the tire iron
but before I could lift it
in threatening manner
a city cop car turned right
onto Lyon from Greenwich

the time was 2:30am

my situation was as if
only conjured up in mind–
a police car pulled up
right next to
two startled bums
as I dropped the tire iron

the policemen got out
and opened the back door
on the driver's side
and pointed

without an ounce of fuss
the two disheveled men
got in
as did the cop
driving off
into what could've been
the fairy tale of me
with a wife and a son
and almost
one more on the way

it was written —no
it happened
just for me

all I had to do was
prepare for a life of ease
but of course
I didn't

I kept fighting off the prospect
of becoming what I'm not
and the life we left to build
remained an empty lot

yet loss is where I'm found
in an plaintive memory
where the past absorbs
the victory of failure

THE OLD BLOCK

my older son —age three
was attending a co-op
where I taught once a week
to offset the tuition, when
picking him up
the teacher explained
they were playing a game
called Change Something
where the kids all sat
around in a circle
then one was picked
to go hide behind a curtain
and change something
about themselves, like
taking off a shoe
or rolling up their pants
then return to the group
and stand in the center
of the circle to allow
the other kids to guess
what they had changed

well, my son Max was picked
he went behind the curtain
and never came back out
so the teacher went around
to find him standing there
arms folded with a scowl

the teacher said to Max
You are supposed
to change something
to which Max replied
I changed my mind

I never worried much
about him ever since

AND THEN I WAS NONE

sitting back on some boxes
containing what was left of my life
I cracked the seal to a pint of scotch

waiting for somebody
I had called with a truck
who would help move my stuff
to a locker

my wife and kids were gone

the mail fell through the slot–
you can be a diesel mechanic
a politician wanting votes
and a phone bill

I folded up the first two
and slid them in my pocket

I tore up the bill
and threw it away

two guys showed up
in a truck that looked as if
Frankenstein might've patched it
from the pieces of other dead trucks
but it did fit all my boxes
so I climbed in between
my new friends
as the engine started
and offered them
a belt of scotch

turned out
they were brothers
and the youngest
reached under
the passenger seat
pulling out a quart
of tequila
which we each
drank from instead

I gave them cash
after they carried my boxes
to the freight elevator
then went in and paid
for my locker

the management team
were newlyweds
freshly moved down
from Alberta
and happy to have the job

I took a unit
on the 4th floor
and rode the elevator up
taking swigs off the scotch

I stacked the boxes
in the locker, and
damn if it didn't
feel cozy

I pulled down the gate
shut off the light
smoked a cigaret
then fell asleep
to be awakened
after dark
when the gate
swung open
and there stood
the manager
saying he was really
sorry I had
no place else to go
but nobody's allowed
to live in their locker
and those were
the rules

outside
I leaned against a wall
listening to the traffic

an old man
sitting at a bus stop
asked me for a cigaret

he seemed alright

I pulled out the pack
and flipped open
the box-top

a lone red filter
stared out
at us both

I handed him the pack

he thanked me kindly
then lit up
and threw
the empty pack
in the gutter

I liked him better
since he littered

I dug my hand down
my front pocket
clutched
my right fist around
the last few bucks
I had left
in the world

up ahead
the flashing neon
above a corner market
reminded me of a face
I hadn't thought of in years

THIS SHOULD MEAN SOMETHING

The face Is Mine
Our days went By
Stop it There
I don't want to Know
It's very Clear
Growing Old
Whether you Recognize
All of this Works
While finding your Dream
Alive Inside
Pain is the Backwash
Get used to It

(one chosen line from thirteen bar napkins scribbles)

THE PAST FROM A BLAST

Wendy and I
were
beyond doubt
romantic
and
San Francisco
was our special
place to be–

October 17, 1989
driving down from Marin
about quarter past 5
on our way to pick up
two World Series tickets
my car gave quite a jolt
on the Golden Gate Bridge
that I thought
was just a clutch
I could ill afford
to fix, but
after pulling up at Lil's
which was packed out front
I went to Billy for the tickets
who told me
The Bay Bridge
collapsed–

we could've easily
been on The Bay Bridge
had we stayed in Alameda
where earlier that morning
we saw a baby egret
walking backwards

on the beach
and while finding this odd
we must've picked up on
its vibe –because
we'd driven to Marin

the bar was closed in case
an aftershock came along
so we bought two bottles
of Chandon at the market
and –popping one each
ambled down Lombard
to check out the Marina
that someone told us
was on fire, though
as soon as the air
hung densely with gas
we turned hand in hand
taking sips back to the store

where we traded
in our empties
and paid for
two more bottles
that we popped
without delay
then headed up
the Lyon Steps
pausing near the top
to admire our view
from the Headlands
to Berkeley, when
this rail-thin guy
with stringy hair
approached us

with an invite
to play the harpsichord
in this mansion nearby
he was helping restore

well
since the gifted Wendy
was a wonderful pianist
we immediately accepted
with a Why the hell not
that is –until he mentioned
the owner's gun collection
and so –thinking better
we politely declined

as the sun went on retreat
we made our trek down
from the Heights
to get more wine
before the store ran out
which they had
–of Chandon
so we were stuck
with Freixenet
but –at that point
who could tell

while on Lyon outside Lil's
the locals brought out tables
soon filled with tasty fare

chairs appeared
and bottles of wine

candles were lit
joints passed around

the guy to my left asked
Do you like Glenlivet
I told him Sure
he said C'mon
where I stood by
until he found it
in the dark

we had a swig
and hit the street

even a police car stopped
to shine its headlights
on the crowd

we knew so little
beyond
the bridge had
collapsed

somehow
this held us closer

everybody there
survived

then the time came
for this night to end
so I drove us back
over the bridge
which inconceivably
hadn't closed

we made a stop
at Vista Point
to catch of view
of San Francisco
all alone there
in the dark
save for
that fire
still burning
the Marina

Wendy soon passed out
once back on the road
so I carried her in
then called my pal Mitch
who had talked to my ex
that he told me had said
There's no way in hell
that son of a bitch's dead

and though my life
had not yet ended
I still knew nothing
of the damage
just lying there
assessing
if this fault
had broken me

BLINDED BY A BARE WHITE WALL

I knew right then
in a stone clear silence

the void was stacked
against the fact
that I would ever belong

there I was on idle, only
more of same not me

I had to move on
to continue to be
which I did with
heavy sadness

I left behind diversion
from not living a life of regret
to preoccupy a hopefulness
that I might have
something to give

not just the past
subjected to
how apt my now
seemed then
though
I never gave way
to self-reproach
once my illusions
converted a home

TO EVERYTHING YOU ARE

I fell for you just now

fell
over your face
as I stared into the mirror
that I set before you
to stare through
as you went inside
the parts you love
most about yourself

I fell into a mirror
where love began
just then

I fell
when then was now

you'll cry
when I stop loving you
because
my love won't stop
until I stop

Friday
September 17th
1993

11:20pm
I fell

A LIFE IN THE DAYS OF A THEATER

we slept on a shelf
overlooking the stage

we didn't have a kitchen
the stage was our stove

from each machination
came a new exploration

fabricating resolve
for the nutriment of all . . .

which takes me on back
to a time in the past

while living in The Marilyn
Monroe Memorial Theater
South of Market
San Francisco
where —always
each vision
prevailed

I had just written Handout–
a play about this homeless man
whose life is transfigured
to a work of corporate art

the action is told
in reverse
(it being)
inspired by
Pinter's Betrayal

the year was 1996
and I was casting
the role of Sheldon
who is described as
"an entry level"

so I basically
needed a stiff
with a dream
to exploit
the textbook
idealist
and I had
someone
in mind

his name was Lance
and he worked at
the coffee shop
not two blocks away
from the theater
who, when I met him
told me –that
more than anything
he wanted to act

alright Lance
here's your chance
and I cast him
as Sheldon
the intern
in Handout

we were two weeks
into rehearsal
and Lance just
couldn't loosen up

he had the first line
in the second act
and no matter
how long we waited
Lance never said it
without my prompt–

ironically
the line was
We're not getting anywhere

one day he was late
when the phone rang
and it was Lance
calling me collect
to say he was still
at work –collect!

I ran around the corner
and watched him
wipe down all the tables
again and again
like life itself would spring
from his actions
but in reality
Lance wasn't just a stiff
he was scared fucking stiff
and had no business ever
setting foot upon a stage

so I had to let him go
but the show went on

even the main critic
from the Chronicle
attended our theater
for the very first time
that opening night

I can't recall
his name now
though maybe
I should google
nah

we packed the house
with many ringers
and were hoping
for the best

even Joie brought
her entire class
for the marginalized
and
mentally challenged

the production
was perfect

so we waited for the critic
to publish his review
and when it came
he had reviewed
another play

with a homeless
protagonist
who hung from a cage
in the middle of this room
to the sound of piped-in bells
but he completely ignored mine

here we were
a little fifty seat theater
putting everything
out on the stage

how bad could his
review have been

I'd gotten
Stay at home and stare
at a wall for an hour

it could not
have been worse
that that

and later on
I got a letter
from one of Joie's students
which read–
Soon as I realized
your play was going
back to front

I knew it was
a great mind-fuck
alas –one
I enjoyed
immensely
so I sent a copy
of this review
to the critic whose name
still escapes me
and said
As soon as I didn't
see your review
I knew it was
a great mind-fuck
alas –one
I never got
the chance
to enjoy

we staged
many more plays
and mistakes
were made
though none
overruled
our creations

then one day
as I stood out
in the vestibule
this girl stopped
and told me

she had been in theater
and now worked
at the coffee shop
around the corner

I chuckled
Not much of a reference
I tried it once with Lance
and from the look on her face
I knew Lance was dead

he had died a ways back
when a cab hit his bike

it might've been
Handout's
opening night

I'd never heard
that he was gone

if only he could have
remembered
his first line
and grown
confidence
from there
yet then
there are those
who attest to
When it's your time
Your time is up

Kathi and I
moved out in 2000
when the landlord
quintupled the rent
yet there in the meantime
we both missed the '90s
while creating worlds
where others
could possibly
belong

UNDER DOG

I'd never have the chance
to express a keener insight
on the foibles of life
than I had right then
so I quickly called
my youngest son
before it slipped away
and soon he answered

I said Dylan
(who was 8)
he dawdled
Yep
I bid
Just Listen
and, solemnly
I gave my all

each word worth
its weight in gold
then pausing
caught my breath
and posed
Do you understand
to silence

Dylan
hey there
Dylan

nothing

finally
tried again
repeating
Do You Understand

he deadpanned
I had the phone
to the dog's ear

how could I be mad
when he was
absolutely right

there wasn't one word
of my broadside that
he had need of to hear

so after telling the kid
next time
give me the dog
we shared a laugh
and parted ways

then I tried hard
to recollect
what all I said
but it was gone

PERFECT O'CLOCK

high praise belongs to
whatever's gone wrong

the coughing
the doubts

ants appear
in the kitchen

a white plastic bag
softly floats
through the air

staying numb
dreaming
night-garbled
might haves

cause
for celebration

each moment
–your friend

TIME FOR A CHANGE

everything
went suddenly black
and there I was
standing before
what looked like
the gates of Heaven
when along came a very
hospitable looking fellow
cradling a white book
speckled with stars

he stood as the gate
swung silently open
then thumbed through the book
and soon beckoned to me
saying Good name –Peter
Same as mine.

St. Peter shut the book
and asked You want in?

I shook my head
emphatically –No

he smiled and told me
I'm glad you said that
Would you mind
If I joined you?

I said Sure

he sighed Thanks, Pete
I'm really bored here

and as we started our descent
he stated Organized Religions
are the killers of souls

giving us much to discuss
on our long journey down

NO MAKE UP DATE

I went into Vesuvio
one mid-afternoon
and ordered a pint of beer
when Lawrence Ferlinghetti
whom I heard
had just turned 80
sat down on the stool
next to me

I nodded my head
and he nodded back
so I proffered You know
the last time this city
had any real bearing
was when all the sailors
returned through the Gate
right after World War II

he looked at me and said
I was one of those sailors

the stage was set

I reached for my beer
which spilled across the bar

his people rushed in
and whisked him away
like I had every plague
in the world

little old me –sitting
sober as a judge, why
I hadn't yet taken
a sip from my glass

heading home –then
I thought
We only get one chance
but, at least
they didn't charge me
for the beer

CHEERS

I was tending bar one night
to a pretty good crowd

there was a jockey of renown
with an entourage of couples
and when George
who used to run the place
came in with Al –who did
it was party time central
until
this kind of lumpy dweeb
took the last empty stool
and started spouting nonsense
as soon as I served him a beer

You know –he suggested
This place is like Cheers
Right?
Cause in Cheers
you gotta guy
who sits at the bar
and says funny things
well I'm like that guy
so this place is like Cheers

which was harmless enough

but when he insulted
a friend of the jockey's wife
I snatched his beer
off the bar and snarled

This place is nothing
like Cheers –because
nobody ever got 86'ed
from there –So now
You get the fuck out

and he stared into the void
for the longest time –then
stood up and walked out
from whence he came

well
some fourteen years later
I walked into Specs
on Thanksgiving night
and told John at the bar
that my mother died
six years ago today
and while John was sympathetic
the lumpy stranger next to him
shot straight at me
She should be dead

I surprisingly held it together
while snapping Look, Asshole
You seem to have more problems
than I can handle at the moment
and made a beeline out the door

then three blocks later
it dawned on me
who
that little shit was–

the Cheers jerk I cut off
that time at the bar

opportunity rang
and he
answered
the bell
fourteen
long years
later

thinking Damn
there I was
seeking solace
from a friend
yet the moment
but enabled
some old grudge
to be avenged
and
climbing
the last hill
I decided
it was time
to move on

BIGGER THAN LIFE

my mom died
after Thanksgiving
so sometimes I see her
as a Macy's float

befuddled revelers
wondering
who this person is

I could try to explain
she was bigger than life
yet also was blinded by
years of abuse
that made her
imperceptive to mine

there she goes passing
tethered until
her being just
faded away

HABIT WITH ME

some twenty years back
freshly moved to New York
while staying at the Cosmo
on Chambers

we decided on a Sunday
during a blizzard
to hock my trumpet
for some badly needed cash

the first place on Church
was a We Buy Gold dump
so I said Kathi Don't Bother
but she went in regardless

as I stood in the snow
by the subway entrance
three nuns walked by
through a half-foot of snow

one of the nuns
broke off from her bunch
to stare into the window
standing next to me

I thought
why the hell would she
stop here in a blizzard
taking her presence as
a personal affront

the next time I looked
she had rejoined her friends
trudging down Church
disappearing in the storm

looking into the store
through cheap strands of gold
I could see the counterman
sadly shaking his head

turning my head back
a glint of green caught my eye
right there at my feet –where
atop the snow sat
much prettier than pleased
a folded fifty dollar bill
and it wasn't alone

I stood back up counting
fifty, another fifty
makes a hundred –and
a ten –only TEN
a hundred and ten
U.S. dollars

I pulled the door open
screeching Kathi Let's Go
thinking
Why did this nun
leave me money on the street
just two weeks from Christmas
and why only ten
with the fifties

laughing with joy
we hit the nearest bar
where our story was good
for a couple of beers
then we broke a fifty
and had a couple more
agreeing on the answer
We Were Home

NOT ALL OF THIS IS BAD

last subway stop
train grinds to halt
as I exit to the front
through the station

the conductor gets off
just steps ahead of me

so feeling a moment
I barked at him
You the conductor?

he answered Yeah
turning slightly

so, somewhat incensed
I chided Six years ago
you shut the doors in my face

and he shrugged I know
Haven't slept well
ever since
and that was that

then we rejoined
the world

THE LADY DOWNSTAIRS

Catherine was her name
and we were neighbors
fourteen years

she lived on the floor below
and always asked me
If I needed anything
and I would always reply
Yes, Catherine
An invite to your
100th birthday party

she made it to 99
having lived there
63 years
and I found out
that her aunt
lived there
before her

she was the best neighbor
we'd ever had
and she said the same
about us

my favorite
of her stories
went–
once back
in the '60s
some thief broke in
her bathroom window

but at the time
she had this dog
that apparently
scared off
the intruder
because
nothing
had been taken
though
the wannabe thief
left these sneakers
in her bathroom
along with broken glass

she swept up the glass
but couldn't figure out
what to do with the sneakers
so she left them on the sill
in case the thief came back
and they just sat there
for a week
which made her feel worse
so she took them downstairs
and left them on the street
right next to the building
if the thief happened by
but the sneakers remained
as did she –at wit's end

so finally
out of options
she tossed them
in the trash
and went
unselfishly
on from there
with her long
and fruitful life
which I, luckily
played a part in
till the end

EVERY CLOUD

my ex-wife died
our younger son
called me crying
perhaps she fell
no one really knew
except on this day
she was gone

she died in Phoenix
where she was born
and I went back
to a time, once
I was looking
for a job
there on
one morning
pushing noon
with her and Max
not quite yet two
both waiting
in the car

I came out of that place
just as unimpressed
as the management
was with me
when off to the left
up the sidewalk
strolled Chrissie Hynde
with her kid

so I slowly
sidled up
with our son
while
playfully bidding
Please
imbue him
with your talents

she shot me an outraged look
lambasting I'm not Jesus Christ

I pulled Jennifer
into the conversation
soothing Chrissie
She's one of your biggest fans
and they talked for a bit
while their kids interacted
as I skulked back to the car

Chrissie asked Jennifer
You wanna see the show

so later on
there we were
and we enjoyed
ourselves
immensely

some things
work out
favorably
however long
they last

so thinking back
to that look she shot
it sure seemed as if
she disregarded
the words out of
any man's mouth
and I realize now
she must be –still
way ahead of her
time

TWO STOOLS DOWN

I was sitting at
the middle of a bar
rewriting some
of my poetry

she was sitting at
the end of same bar
writing, too

she leaned my way
with no one betweeen
and asked me
what are you doing

I said
Working on a poem
You?

She answered
Same

and right smack there
from that point on
we became
creative partners

30 years later
we are still
writing poems

30 years later
we are still

FOR
WHEN THIS
MOURNFUL ROAD
ABRUPTLY
ENDS

every single day
the media squeals
Ten
Shot Dead
At The
Local Mall
and
there wasn't
a bad bone
amongst
them

though the killers
are revealed
a bit more
complex

first
the family
avows
they never
saw this
coming
then
their
co-workers
admit

we didn't know
they were
so flawed
and
each victim
remains
this
pillar of hope
full of
fountains
of dreams
unconditionally
loved
by all

not only their kids
and their own step kids
but even their ex's step kids

now I've lived with our lot
getting on past sixty years
and it's rare
when you cross paths
with one virtuous soul

most are
clutching theirs
on top of
coveting
what's mine

even
thoughts and prayers

so
if that's
how I go

(as a mass shooting victim)

let it be
known
how I'd like
my testament
to read

"Most of the people who knew him
were surprised he wasn't the shooter"

or
better still

(whatever my end might be)

"He was so far ahead of his time
that maybe it will have the chance
to catch up now since he's gone"

I PAID MY RENT

what's the use of caviling
I was born maladjusted
not only because
there's been war everyday

since one kind took the throne
over others bought and sold

some explain –some explode
reinventing more injustice

our kind is mankind
and the scales
have never balanced

even the solution
is part of the problem
and any way of thinking
is to blame for what is wrong

if only one day
would leave me at ease
from the past's need to haunt
what the present wants to cancel
while the future only bodes
the bare promise of more haunting

I came right down that dark canal
to join this world all ill-equipped
insomuch as to but think

that when this is all over
even the void
will be stacked up
against me
but therein
lies the rub
for in the end
we all are equal

I was born maladjusted
the very best that I could be
and the moment my time's over
my next month's rent will be dirt cheap

ABOUT PETER CARLAFTES

Peter Carlaftes is author of numerous books including the poetry collections *Drunkyard Dog* and *I Fold With the Hand I Was Dealt* and two collections of plays: *Teatrophy* and *Triumph for Rent.* He is co-editor of the annual contemporary dada journal, *Maintenant,* co-editor of three editions of the *Have a NYC: New York Stories* series, and editor of *The Faking of the President: Nineteen Stories of White House Noir.* His poetry has recently appeared in *A Shape Produced by a Curve, NYC from the Inside, Love, Love, Chorus: A Literary Mixtape,* and many more journals and anthologies. He is co-director of Three Rooms Press.

RECENT AND FORTHCOMING BOOKS FROM THREE ROOMS PRESS

FICTION

Lucy Jane Bledsoe
No Stopping Us Now

Rishab Borah
The Door to Inferna

Meagan Brothers
Weird Girl and What's His Name

Christopher Chambers
Scavenger
Standalone

Ebele Chizea
Aquarian Dawn

Ron Dakron
Hello Devilfish!

Robert Duncan
Loudmouth

Michael T. Fournier
Hidden Wheel
Swing State

Aaron Hamburger
Nirvana Is Here

William Least Heat-Moon
Celestial Mechanics

Aimee Herman
Everything Grows

Kelly Ann Jacobson
Tink and Wendy
Robin and Her Misfits

Jethro K. Lieberman
Everything Is Jake

Eamon Loingsigh
Light of the Diddicoy
Exile on Bridge Street

John Marshall
The Greenfather

Alvin Orloff
Vulgarian Rhapsody

Micki Ravizee
Of Blood and Lightning

Aram Saroyan
Still Night in L.A.

Robert Silverberg
The Face of the Waters

Stephen Spotte
Animal Wrongs

Richard Vetere
The Writers Afterlife
Champagne and Cocaine

Jessamyn Violet
Secret Rules to Being a Rockstar

Julia Watts
Quiver
Needlework
Lovesick Blossoms

Gina Yates
Narcissus Nobody

MEMOIR & BIOGRAPHY

Nassrine Azimi and Michel Wasserman
Last Boat to Yokohama: The Life and Legacy of Beate Sirota Gordon

William S. Burroughs & Allen Ginsberg
Don't Hide the Madness: William S. Burroughs in Conversation with Allen Ginsberg
edited by Steven Taylor

James Carr
BAD: The Autobiography of James Carr

Judy Gumbo
Yippie Girl: Exploits in Protest and Defeating the FBI

Judith Malina
Full Moon Stages: Personal Notes from 50 Years of The Living Theatre

Phil Marcade
Punk Avenue: Inside the New York City Underground, 1972–1982

Jillian Marshall
Japanthem: Counter-Cultural Experiences; Cross-Cultural Remixes

Alvin Orloff
Disasterama! Adventures in the Queer Underground 1977–1997

Nicca Ray
Ray by Ray: A Daughter's Take on the Legend of Nicholas Ray

Stephen Spotte
My Watery Self: Memoirs of a Marine Scientist

PHOTOGRAPHY-MEMOIR

Mike Watt
On & Off Bass

SHORT STORY ANTHOLOGIES

SINGLE AUTHOR

Alien Archives: Stories
by Robert Silverberg

First-Person Singularities: Stories
by Robert Silverberg
with an introduction by John Scalzi

Tales from the Eternal Café: Stories
by Janet Hamill, with an introduction
by Patti Smith

Time and Time Again: Sixteen Trips in Time
by Robert Silverberg

The Unvarnished Gary Phillips: A Mondo Pulp Collection
by Gary Phillips

Voyagers: Twelve Journeys in Space and Time
by Robert Silverberg

MULTI-AUTHOR

Crime + Music: Twenty Stories of Music-Themed Noir
edited by Jim Fusilli

Dark City Lights: New York Stories
edited by Lawrence Block

The Faking of the President: Twenty Stories of White House Noir
edited by Peter Carlaftes

Florida Happens: Bouchercon 2018 Anthology
edited by Greg Herren

Have a NYC I, II & III: New York Short Stories;
edited by Peter Carlaftes
& Kat Georges

No Body, No Crime: Twenty-two Tales of Taylor Swift-Inspired Noir
edited by Alex Segura & Joe Clifford

Songs of My Selfie: An Anthology of Millennial Stories
edited by Constance Renfrow

The Obama Inheritance: 15 Stories of Conspiracy Noir
edited by Gary Phillips

This Way to the End Times: Classic and New Stories of the Apocalypse
edited by Robert Silverberg

MIXED MEDIA

John S. Paul
Sign Language: A Painter's Notebook
(photography, poetry and prose)

DADA

Maintenant: A Journal of Contemporary Dada Writing & Art
(annual, since 2008)

HUMOR

Peter Carlaftes
A Year on Facebook

FILM & PLAYS

Israel Horovitz
My Old Lady: Complete Stage Play and Screenplay with an Essay on Adaptation

Peter Carlaftes
Triumph For Rent (3 Plays)
Teatrophy (3 More Plays)

Kat Georges
Three Somebodies: Plays about Notorious Dissidents

TRANSLATIONS

Thomas Bernhard
On Earth and in Hell
(poems of Thomas Bernhard with English translations by Peter Waugh)

Patrizia Gattaceca
Isula d'Anima / Soul Island

César Vallejo | Gerard Malanga
Malanga Chasing Vallejo
(selected poems of César Vallejo with English translations and additional notes by Gerard Malanga)

George Wallace
EOS: Abductor of Men
(selected poems in Greek & English)

ESSAYS

Richard Katrovas
Raising Girls in Bohemia: Meditations of an American Father

Far Away From Close to Home
Vanessa Baden Kelly

Womentality: Thirteen Empowering Stories by Everyday Women Who Said Goodbye to the Workplace and Hello to Their Lives
edited by Erin Wildermuth

POETRY COLLECTIONS

Hala Alyan
Atrium

Peter Carlaftes
DrunkYard Dog
I Fold with the Hand I Was Dealt
Life in the Past Lane

Thomas Fucaloro
It Starts from the Belly and Blooms

Kat Georges
Our Lady of the Hunger
Awe and Other Words Like Wow

Robert Gibbons
Close to the Tree

Israel Horovitz
Heaven and Other Poems

David Lawton
Sharp Blue Stream

Jane LeCroy
Signature Play

Philip Meersman
This Is Belgian Chocolate

Jane Ormerod
Recreational Vehicles on Fire
Welcome to the Museum of Cattle

Lisa Panepinto
On This Borrowed Bike

George Wallace
Poppin' Johnny

Three Rooms Press | New York, NY | Current Catalog: www.threeroomspress.com
Three Rooms Press books are distributed by Publishers Group West: www.pgw.com